What readers are saying

These poems originate from a heart full of love for both nature and human beings, what a wonderful human she is herself.

-Dr. Helen Caldicott

In War Poems, Mimi German's compassion and heartbreak shine clearly through the carnage. A Jew who refuses the easy out of taking sides, she stands with her hands and her heart open to Arab and Jew alike—to all who are human, and to their suffering. She finds both beauty and horror in the first 100 days of a reality we would all rather ignore, and in so doing, she helps us to not look away.

-Rabbi Ariel Stone, Temple Shir Tikvah, Portland

The War Poems is a priceless meditation on the effect of war, even on those far from battle. The poems encourage us to consider not just the suffering of war, but the cost to our souls.

-Pastor Steven Kimes

When there was a roaring silence from so many, these poems comforted and companioned me with their ability to hold a moment, to look at a shard of glass with all lights reflecting through. They have helped me process the grief and shock of the latest war in the Middle East, through the continuing escalation in Gaza, through the sometimes inexplicable reaction of various nations. Thank you, Mimi, for your courage, your humanity, your search for truth, your dedication to this world.

During the first hundred days of Israel's assault on Gaza after the Hamas attack on Israel on October 7, 2023, Mimi German posted a poem a day. These daily meditations express tenderness, balance, and empathy for all who suffer and for the impermanent beauties of (even) blood-soaked moments.

-K. Kendall, Ph.D., retired professor of Theatre and English.

"Mimi German's War Poems bring the unfathomable out of the shadows and into the clear light of truth. With her 100 poetic meditations, which ring like sounding bells, she leads us through the darkness and into the open expanse of what peace between all people could be."

-Amy Rodriguez, Artist

An Opus ! in its own *write* & truly rewarding!

-John Bertucci, Peace and Anti-nuclear Activist

Les poèmes de Mimi German entremêlent les merveilles de la nature et les horreurs contre nature de l'homme. Dans ce recueil étonnant, elle nous rappelle que tout le monde perd à la guerre, la planète et ses habitants. Alors qu'elle juxtapose, une beauté qui a été et qui pourrait encore être - un bédouin à la tente ouverte et accueillante, un fruit de sabre offrant un jus sucré à quiconque, sans distinction de race de la race, de la croyance et de la couleur. War Poems est un regard candide un regard franc, teinté d'optimisme, sur ce qui pourrait advenir si nous sortions de l'autre côté de ces batailles sans fin.

- **Michael D. Amitin International** Poet Laureate Paris, Fr

In crisis, each of us hopes to respond with whatever strengths we have at our disposal. In the case of a poet, in the case of Mimi German, that tool is poetry. As soon as the war began, she took pen to hand. Although the war is geographically a world away, for Mimi, an American Jew, the carnage might as well be raging right just outside her door in the high deserts of Eastern Oregon.

Through her art, Mimi explores the grief, searches for beauty, and advocates for peace. Day by day by day.

-**Kelly Lou O'Hanley**, friend and sometimes editor of The War Poems

Mimi's war poems helped me process emotionally the horrific and unfolding slaughter in Israel and Gaza. They inspired me to learn more about the century old conflict and write music. The poems have been sometimes challenging, sometimes uplifting, and always meaningful.

-Dan Kaufman, Activist, PDXK Productions, Dan Kaufman Band. Portland, Oregon

In what started out as a personal exploration of feelings and trying to make sense of why there is no peace, Mimi traces her own ancestral roots, and the history of the region in an attempt to explain why this type of conflict exists.

Deborah Tosun Kilday, Founder/Owner/CEO National Beat Poetry Foundation, Inc.

Mimi has grabbed hold of a chord and will not let go... There are so many lines worth memorizing.

-Larry Jaffe, Poet in Residence at Jack Kerouac House

During a time when the most far-right government in Israel's history has been found guilty of a plausible case of genocide in Gaza by the International Court of Justice, it seems crucial for Jewish and other poets to present alternative visions, visions for peace, for Israel and Palestine. As a longtime poet and peace activist, Mimi German has the literary skills and political experience to address these urgent and complicated times. Her war poems—really, peace poems—are humane, thought-provoking, philosophically deep, and filled with the kind of astonishing, "aha" phrasings that Emily Dickinson said were the ingredients needed to create powerful and memorable poetry: "war can be heard in the silence of death"; "a genocide to which they've cheered l'chaim"; "the game of revenge / ends in nightmares"; "we all have forgotten never to forget." While also mourning Israeli victims of the terrible 10/7 Hamas attacks, and pages before explicitly criticizing the extremist, hawkish Israeli Prime Minister Netanyahu, German writes: "without anasthesia / let us hear the truth / about war." And in these pages, she offers nonviolent truths ("how does one sleep / when the pillows of justice / are covered in bloodshed") and truth-truce poems in ways that could hopefully warm even the coldest of hearts.

-**Eliot Katz**, Poet and author of The Poetry and Politics of Allen Ginsberg

One hundred poems in 100 days, no misses. That is a major project all by itself but then to publish it...that is courageous. Mimi German's heart lies in an Israel of peaceful coexistence which she has fought for and has had to watch slip away. Her narrative images are charged with that pain and longing. This is no curated collection, it is more of a diary. This book is however a deep look into a heart full of love and sorrow. It is raw and it is brave.

-Malcolm Chaddock, Veterans For Peace, Oregon

Mimi German's newest collection – War Poems/ Israeli-Gaza: The First 100 Days of Carnage – is a powerful song birthed in the emotional desert of war. This lament, a-poem-a-day since October 7, 2023, rises into the air as a call for peace and unity. German writes, in these times of division, with great courage. She writes, as she says in the prologue, as a Jew who lives in the diaspora yet "knows the scent and taste of Israel". And she writes as a person "indivisible". She bears witness to "All who suffer" from this latest Middle East tragedy. German's style of writing lays the soul and the emotions bare. These poems – those brief and those longer – are stripped back, concise and carefully descriptive with striking imagery and metaphor.

Written without punctuation, and mostly without capitalization, they are small and heart-breakingly poignant, large and generously encompassing; they are, by turns, memoir, dream, remembrance, elegy, and eulogy; they take hope in nature's presence and balm. They record the day-to-day thoughts of German including the day-to-day escalation and horror, the feelings of desperation and powerlessness, the hopes and the desolation. This beautiful collective work begs the world for peace and understanding, an end to war, and implores us "to engage in love".

War Poem #35:

"…/how does one sleep / in the searing divisions of a nation / created for survival /

how does one sleep / after the cries of babies / are silenced by grenades / …how

does one sleep / when sorrow is the sunrise / and terror the rising moon".

War Poem #30:

/" the desert air is dry / …it does not pretend to be a savior / … but … / it will provide

/ sails to navigate / the waters of the soul."

I laud both the means and the goal of War Poems. German succeeds in bearing witness, in giving hope, solace, and shared grief. This collection begins the process of healing and love. It functioned for me as a kind of Lectio Divina, in the Christian tradition of spiritual reading, meditation and prayer. These poems, these words, rise from war-infested days; the whole rises like leavened bread. And we must listen, if we thirst for peace, if we hunger for unity. As German writes, "In the name of

humanity / …let us forgive and let go / and never more / raise arms / in war".

- **Laura Grevel**, Poet, Austria

This book of war poems by Mimi German is powerful and punchy — carries weight and authority, not only because the poet herself is a Jew, but also because of her deep compassion and empathy with the victims and survivors of war. The first 100 days of what we, the world, are living through is written here in graphic detail, pulling no punches. "war is poverty of the mind" - a mere six words conveying what war is. "if the trunk of even the oldest olive tree is cut down it will not die" - hope in the air. "to write the unspeakable to bring my horror to the page"

- Mimi German does not shirk from the stark reality of this genocide – her words are sharp, and will linger long after her book is put down. "bodies compost the land" - "i cannot tell yesterday from today" - she is bearing witness as if she is there – the poignancy of her words is palpable. "war is just a missed opportunity for peace" - sage advice indeed. Mimi's last line "what have we become?" - world leaders take note. This book of poems – one for each of the first 100 days – is a valuable contribution to the body of literature on this terrible period in our living history – the pen is always mightier than the sword, and these poems are a tour de force.

-Margaret O'Regan, Irish Activist Poet

War Poems

Israel-Gaza: The First 100 Days of Carnage

by

Mimi German

PUBLISH

EYEPUBLISHEWE

PUBLISHING POETRY, LITERATURE, ART, MUSIC

FOR HUMANITY'S SAKE

A BRAND NEW PUBLISHING COMPANY

SAN FRANCISCO

FOUNDED 2020

this book is dedicated

to Peace

Prologue

On October 7, 2023, I was devastated by the news that Hamas had attacked Israel, killed over one thousand people, and had taken hundreds hostage. My thoughts drifted very quickly to how devastating the revenge would be by the State of Israel in Gaza. As a Jew living in the diaspora, a Jew who knows the scent and taste of Israel, a Jew who speaks the language of Israel, a Jew who loves the land, I have lost my direction home. Each morning, upon awakening, I have tried not only to stare down the horror of what Hamas did, but also the devastation of Israel's retaliatory response - actions it has been waiting to execute for a very long time from this government.

By writing these poems for each of the first 100 days of the war, I bear witness. Not to one side or the other, but to all who suffer from this war. Sometimes, this is the only response to such atrocities. Divisions create the groundwork for war. I am *indivisible*. I am a poet, writing. Writing with the hope of peace and unity and a desire for an immediate end to war in Israel and Gaza.

Table of Contents

War Poem #1

war

is poverty

of the mind

War Poem #2

war

is the malnourished

heart

Mimi German

War Poem #3

a mantra to help me remember who i am

in this time

of war

*

i

love

and within

this spirit

i

live

War Poem #4

how much does it cost
to wage love

Mimi German

War Poem #5

war roams beneath the bared souls of flowers

war surrounds the heart like a tumor

war can be heard in the silence of death

war wears the petals of a child's eyes forever closed

war spatters blood on the leaves of eucalyptus trees

war harvests misery

war is a broken ladder on either side

war is the baker making loaves for the hungry

war is the mother holding tightly to thorns

war is the scent of burning breath

war is not a revolution

war is not a revelation

war is cowardice in the face of love

war is a terrorist

war is the dog chasing its tail

war is a drifter looking for a dime

war is not for lovers

war feasts on love

war meandered into our gardens and never left

War Poem #6

and yet
some still believe
in god

Mimi German

War Poem #7

with nothing left
they make ovens
from sand and dirt
to feed each other
bread

War Poem #8

beyond its highest peak

the mountain rises

fear grounds

in the swirl of war

between them

love ripples   submerged

Mimi German

War Poem #9

*

i do
not resist
i open
in the exhale
to exist

War Poem #10

*

what exists
in the hours of no longer

infinite loss
and the governments parlay

the back and forth of the broom

leaves blow to the curb
then cross blood-stained streets

we've snuffed the candles
no miracles
today
in the formidable play
of whose side of the street are you on
anyway

Mimi German

War Poem #11

between borders
the desert mountains purple before the sun
nubian ibex edge into twilight
feeding into the awe

War Poem #12

*

vining bougainvillea
follow no borders

Mimi German

War Poem #13

dahab

the red sea

lips salting my skin

across the water

saudi arabia

behind me

mountains with roots that berry

in deserts of age

the sound of the oud

a bedouin family takes me

into the language of the heart

the sea is quiet

camels drape the land

with morning

War Poem #14

i've sat among arab villagers

    along the sea

        drinking tea

            eating dried fruits

praying with story and laughter

for each other's survival

Mimi German

War Poem #15

widows gather
like keys on a typewriter
over graves
and flowers

War Poem #16

beneath the rubble
petals flower

deals are made
in lies

grandmother shields
a child's eyes
from the glare of inhumanity

Mimi German

War Poem #17

(L'Chaim)

 who is allowed to live

and who to smell jasmine in the northern hills

to drink mint tea in the sinai

or rejoice in Jerusalem

where on god's green earth exists

not a prison for the poor

the war machine revs its hi$$$

the precipice tumbles

politicians clamor over strategies to kill while

negotiating the innocence of a child

in a genocide to which they've cheered

l'chaim

War Poem #18

the moon comes up from the margins

lighting its way into consciousness

on earth

a once revered and holy planet

now just a place

to bury the dead

and sweep into the sea

      ashes of war

Mimi German

War Poem #19

if i could sit with you
i would bring you bread
and tea with rumaanim
felafel and warm pita
and gifts for your family

if
is such an empty word
resigning itself to failure

War Poem #20

leaves blow down from their trees

crossing fields and hoof prints of deer

up the coyote trail past the quail

i watch them traverse this desert landscape

driven this way and then

beyond my sight

where all I can feel

is their fear in the silence

between the gnashing teeth of bombs

Mimi German

War Poem #21

i've counted the seeds of the rimon

in each seed

a voice

a mantra

of love

compassion

and a warning

War Poem #22

Mimi German

War Poem #23

yesterday's poem

was just

silence

        on the page

War Poem #24

daybreak slices its way

like a candied layer cake

across the desert sky

one might think

that all is well

in the world

the trees in the pardes birthed

farmers harvested fruit

pies were made

peaches canned

the first frost is now days old

but I still have not

put a mezuzah on our door

Mimi German

War Poem #25

i have burned
all the propaganda
beneath moons
of bloodshed

for love

War Poem #26

if the trunk of
the oldest olive tree
is cut down
it will not die

from its roots
shoots rise up
ensuring its existence

and from the shatter
of hearts

       seeds

Mimi German

War Poem #27

without anesthesia
let us hear the truth

about war

War Poem #28

this big coyote
walks across the field

turns at the stand of trees
takes a few long steps
sniffs the wind

crosses over
in the secrecy of grasses
for the hen house

Mimi German

War Poem #29

we wait

for no one

is coming

War Poem #30

the desert air is dry
it does not pretend
to be a savior

or hear sorrow
or wet the wadis
with your tears

but if you are still
in the heat of its winds
it will provide
sails to navigate
the waters of the soul

Mimi German

War Poem #31

it's been 31 days since

War Poem #32

to write the unspeakable

to bring

my horror

to the page

              dare i

this merry-go-round

      of war

a child for a child

black smoke

billows toward

no one's heaven

Mimi German

War Poem #33

war

is not

a metaphor

War Poem #34

in oneness
transcendence
of dueling narratives

Mimi German

War Poem #35

how does one sleep
on rubble and ash
on the sharp edge
of fear

how does one sleep
waiting for answers
from the dead

how does one sleep
in the searing divisions of a nation
created for survival

how does one sleep
after the cries of babies
are silenced by grenades

how does one sleep
after walking through
the mutilation of a dream

how does one sleep
when the pillows of justice
are covered in bloodshed

how does one sleep
when sorrow is the sunrise
and terror the rising moon

War Poem #36

(peace offering dream)

i plait november's red willows
into my greying hair
crouch then crawl
inside the desert's holy waters
where a fallen bough
of juniper curls naked to my waist
then into the blue of early evening light

high at the mountain's peak
upon the footsteps of the ages
rock of sages and breath
of wild ram and sallow tongue
of snake and faraway draw
i lay down my body's gown
of magpie   of coyote
singing their sonata
such a wild sky
i offer my soul to join

Mimi German

we sing for mercy for peace for love

to no one at all who hear

how the gods were never

and for the living

only the tortured remnants of ghosts

remain

War Poem #37

place your burden

and yours

and yes

yours

all the sorrow

tears scars blood

all the devastation

of war and longing

for peace

into this basket

of pomegranate seeds

woven in fractals of flowers

let us mix them

then spill to earth

these burdens

Mimi German

that all the burdens

are one burden

a collective burden

undifferentiated

by place or culture

but the burden

belonging to all of humanity

War Poem #38

in the name of rachel corrie

in the name of ahed tamimi

in the name of israeli mothers

in the name of palestinian mothers

in the name of all the children

cease fire now

in the name of humanity

let us bow down before sanity

like abraham did before the people

so that he could bury his wife

so that we may bury this war

so that we can forgive

traumas we've carried

since gods became mortals

Mimi German

for the sake of the living
for the wail of the wolf
for the tender buds of spring
let us forgive and let go

lift this fog from the rivers
shine a light so bright that all soldiers find their souls
a light so candescent that governments can hide
nothing
a light so fierce that shadows cease
a light so radiant it blinds all hatred

i toss these seeds

to the unfair winds

to heal

to bury the dead

to care for the living

to mend our hearts

to remember our breath

to engage in love

to love

to love

to love

and never more

raise arms

in war

Mimi German

War Poem #39

children
how I weep the weight
of what would have been
this season's olive harvest

none emerge
who know the curatives
for this impermanence of peace

so i must cure my own
in your name
from the salt of my tears
and the briny muscle of my heart
and in your name
i will plant young trees of olive
of fig of carob of lemon
bare rooted all
as is my soul

beside it i will toss seeds of barley

to earth to earth

then braid challah

from grain sprouting in your name

for shabbat for the healing

that must come

for love for unity

that may not ever grow

Mimi German

War Poem #40

rage turns

    to flame

        flowering

in the spinning

    splintered wheels

        of desperation

the swelter

    the swale

        of divide

War Poem #41

*

in the distance
the mountain's trees
change color before becoming
the moon

Mimi German

War Poem #42

(Galilee Fumitory, an extremely rare flower in Israel's Hanita Forest near Lebanon)

did you mean by saying
from the river to the sea
that you yearn to discover
the flowering path

that you have seen
the wild tulips hatch
upon the northern hills
and spotted the rarest flower
like a violet-colored peace
so extremely rare
seen by too few to believe
it could be real

when you saw the flowering lily

felt its petals in your soul

that light and grace grow plentiful

from the hills of galilee

south into the sea

did it show you that of flowers

all are we

i'm certain this must be

what you meant when you said

from the river to the sea

of flowers all are we

of flowers all are we

Mimi German

War Poem #43

i wonder
how you pray
when the adhan summons you
to kneel
in the rubble of broken bones
your people

i wonder
how i can recite the sh'ma
when terror reigns from abroad
but also from within

War Poem #44

oh war, how seductive your lines

how you curve like a stripper

as your slink collects dollars

in the crimp of your bodice

from degenerate minds

the stench of oil men

and arms dealers

who in their giddy

sell you bombs

and peace

how dare you sit

in the corner of the bar

emanating illusions

too elusive to grasp

while the dance moves of generals

cause the deaths of thousands

Mimi German

War Poem #45

like leaves falling

from trees

they come home

differently contoured

fractured and torn

in the war game

pawns for terror

all

War Poem #46

upon your return home
joyless candles sputter

by their listless flame
you are told of the deaths
of your mothers and fathers

Mimi German

War Poem #47

between the cactus and the sun
the mountain

War Poem #48

let us cross this chasm

with harvest's heavy branches bending

so that olives

      not blood

may spill upon the land

in this bittersweet morning

lit in anguished light

Mimi German

War Poem #49

is the color of a sunrise red
or is it really an epiphany

go on thinking you know
how it is
how to get there
when there is only one path
and you can't see
that you aren't on it

War Poem #50

i write today as a jew

as this is as much of who i am

as the sky is blue on a summer's day

these poems

each one

are for all

even you

and especially, you

b'shalom b'salam b'yachad

in peace together

Mimi German

War Poem #51

to Netanyahu

as the leaf knows when to sprout
and the sun where to set
you knew these rains were coming
with the thunderclap of martyrs

as god was your witness
as the desert sands blew
you knew that the gates of hemlock
would be breached
your preoccupied stray of heart
this quasi cause of war not peace

the fate from hubris falls upon you
like boulders from the sky
as for the nightmares you have borne
we are forever stained
for what you knew but didn't do
we will expel you and your name

War Poem #52

the generals toss their dice

and clink their coins

in the tattered pockets

of their unholy souls

the numbers of the dead

reveal revenge

hate is greater than the sword

ploughshares turn the dusty soil

bodies compost the land

Mimi German

War Poem #53

sh'mati

i hear you

through your implausible denial

yes the truth is sometimes

too much to bear

so instead

you repudiate its very existence

yet it continues to bare all

even the brunt of it

pushing shadow into light

doesn't it

War Poem #54

i dreamed the airplanes dropped

poems to the people

that said something

about a truce

Mimi German

War Poem #55

as it has been reported

there will be a decisive battle

that could decide

the fate of this war

but what shall be the fate

of the flowers

may the clouds part

for the innocent

and the gods redeem

life's memberships

to all who wield the sword

in this slaughter by the sea

War Poem #56

to the apples in the orchard
please forgive
that i have let you tumble

that i could not
catch you
when you fell into night

you rolled to the fences
then spoiled in darkness
your core softening in dreamlessness

my arms are not wide enough
to become the tree
upon which you turned sweet

my roots uproot
under the skyless dome
of grief

Mimi German

War Poem #57

Edict

by my authority
as a human being
witnessing war crimes

i call
upon all governments
around the world

to refuse
to accept
all US imports

until
Biden shuts down
all permissions for this war

War Poem #58

in amalek they mow the lawn   in the shatter of mirrors
at the river's edge   the fish are belly up   the flowers all
dead   o how this indiscriminate rain has fallen   paper
tigers caught in spider webs crumble in the rubble   you
say tomato i say tomato   humanity effaced there is
nowhere to go

Mimi German

War Poem #59

i cannot tell
yesterday from today

War Poem #60

larry and i have been talking
about how although we are not religious
        neither of us
we're still jews

can't wipe it off
shit   genetically i carry the taysachs gene

so yes
as a poet and as a jew
i think about the future a lot
about 45 becoming 47
about bibi causing unspeakable harm to all
about hamas and the hostages

and what that will mean for me
and larry

as much as i think
about writing this 60th
        war poem

i know you will come for us
and we   me and larry
will be writing poems of your coming

your hatred of us
        jews
is so great that you say you'd rather
a fascist reload in the white house

Mimi German

so to all who are busy grinding
the rabid spittle toward all
                    jews
for what the israeli govt is doing

don't worry
you'll have your turn too

against us   jews

but we poets
me and larry   and all the other jewish poets

will wield the pen to your swords
because what else can we do

War Poem #61

the garden is frozen
    naked and cold

leaves gather
    but never in the right place

flowers fold into frost
    as if in prayer

not even the sun
    can warm this earth

this season of death

Mimi German

War Poem #62

so much powerlessness
in the chambers
these days

we're taking down fence posts
rolling up the wire
freeing the land
to the deer

in my quaker high school
i learned about zen koans
you know
if a tree falls in the forest
etc

in the crush
of despair
and olives left on unfertile ground
is there is time to tend
the mitzvot

will anybody hear

War Poem #63

we did roll up the fences
and the deer did come in
as if on cue as they do
each time we remove
another border

they ate from the fields
beneath the setting
of the pink petaled sun

as the deer ready to bed down
on this fourth night of chanukah
on their soft beds of grasses
bombs drop on gaza
and another family ceases to exist

i don't care about miracles of light
where are there miracles of peace

Mimi German

War Poem #64

the dreidel spins
on its pointed tip
how far it will fall
nobody knows

War Poem #65

they say it is apocalyptic

petals torn off the flowers
rivers running hungry
red in the stink

pieces of the sun
were found beneath rubble
its warmth cold

a bombed out crater
a burial ground
for the future

in israel they collect
sperm from dead soldiers
to rebirth militias

if i close my eyes
then what

Mimi German

War Poem #66

constellations

will always be

just chance alignments

of stars with mythological identities

like the tribes of isaac and ishmael

War Poem #67

i step into the mikvah of memory
the sweet scented hills
of mint of thyme
surrounding the city

                         o yerushalayim

the quarries of stone
that built the temple
became cisterns
to hold the holy waters

                         of life

for a people to exist
and to have suffered
for so long in war
we must never forget

                         love

Mimi German

War Poem #68

(for Yotan, Haim, and Samer)

they waved a white flag

    yet perished

        in a deafening rain

            of what militaries call

                friendly fire

my heart thunders

    in barren tundra

        frozen to the clothespins

            of sorrow

War Poem #69

the clothesline frays
from the weight of frost ·
and frozen barbs

rabbits scatter
from fence post to tree
hiding from the great horns
of owls

in the fog of clouds
coyotes hover
singing songs of catching prey

the sun is on the run
and in the house of war
the chairs are empty
and the tables have been turned

Mimi German

War Poem #70

amid the shifting sands
the mountain stands finite
death infinite and unyielding

War Poem #71

1987

i remember so clearly walking the wadi

it was some miles from jerusalem

using the water from my canteen

i spilled a little on desert flowers

on the dust of dry earth

with too little on my tongue

and although i suffered for it

i'd do it again

because sometimes

we must feed our place

the oneness of it all

and hope

that a tree

grows even in the drought

of peace

Mimi German

War Poem #72

i can't find my way

in your darkness

nor yours

      or yours

mine is a divergent path

tho' wholly connected to the vine

where zahroor berries

break through sinai rock

to be eaten by the wanderer

in search of peace

War Poem #73

at what point
      i'd ask

as if anyone could
possibly know

      is enough

           enough

Mimi German

War Poem #74

if war
saw its reflection
then shattered
in shame

War Poem #75
(for D.T.K.)

i found humanity

grace and purity of heart

in one who grew up

with no religion

Mimi German

War Poem #76

we pledge allegiance to the burning
flag of this nation where we feed each
other thorns mixed with sugar plums
then swallow it down with a cup of life
while allowing our generals and
henchmen to abstain from voting for
immediate aid for a nation it has
decimated with its chocolate petal
covered bombs

War Poem #77

sitting here in the dark
on the first night of winter
the 77th day of war
the wood stove warm
the wind strong
the fog thick
and i don't know
what to think

there used to be seasons
of snow drifts
or sweet scattered petals
of hyacinths
then sand bars to reach
while holding on
to grandfather's hand

my mother tells me
she wants me to be unafraid
        of being a jew
but that was when
there was a place for us
if seasons failed us

Mimi German

it turns out
we failed the seasons
ransacking the fields
that grow children
slashing the rucksack of futures
for you dear palestinians
and for us

i scour the hard ground for roots
leading into some less oppressive past
the winds blow heavy down from the hills
my footprints disappear into the canyons

War Poem #78

a jew sits in bethlehem

    the house of bread

        reading a poem

o wayfarers

i open

my tent

to you   come in   come in

allow me to wash your feet

as my father abraham

did in the days of old

let me clean your face

of dust and blood and tears

for i have heard your cries

Mimi German

come inside

away from the chaos of wars

and eat these loaves of love

i have leavened for you

stay if you like and let us grow

groves of figs and pomegranates

forging a new path with the holy seeds of unity

War Poem #79

(Christmas)

gentle dawn of colors spewn

and cast like orphans to the sky

beneath your gaze

we wait to see

a border lifted

an orchard ripe

a child's laugh

a songbird's song

the drip and slurp of life

Mimi German

War Poem #80

i did not know you
in the sunlight of morning
at the edge of the sea

but i miss you
and long for you

i carry threads made of petals
to begin the mending
the darning of souls

we will fray the borders by the shore
so they will part
where together we will walk
on soft sands and salty waters
where in the antiquity
      of us
we will remember

          laughter

War Poem #81

in your names

      dear dying children

people shout

for the birds to be freed

the cages opened

with such righteous indignation

only suitable for youth

whose lack of awareness of history

is as a dumpster fire

and they will vote for a dictator

to replace the war lord

posing as a christian

in the white house

Mimi German

he will then
come for me
one who really does bewail
your plight

i love you
and i am sorry
that neither justice or equality fit
on the scales of earth
or love

War Poem #82

in this obscurity of light
i can only dream you
        into being
the colors of golden almonds
warming in the groves
and in spring
        fig sweet your tenderness

once you were merely mortal
playing with dolls

this fog masks the true colors
of grasses where bodies tangle
enmeshed in love
by death

even the goats have bleated their way
from the pen into the crush
of concrete

there is no hiding
even in dreams
now that all that exists
is thunder and shadows

Mimi German

War Poem #83

war is just

a missed opportunity
for peace

War Poem #84

*For Judih Weinstein Haggai 1953 - Oct. 7, 2023, Kibbutz Nir
Oz*

i heard about your death
last night

the fog has encroached
and is suffocating my heart

you wrote in one haiku
of *darkening skies and the howls*
of coyotes

i know those coyotes
and i know that sentiment

i hear in the soft sweetness
of your voice
       a friend
as you read your poetry
suffusing our despair with ripe figs

i sorrow over your death

at the steps of your house
       on the land
i leave a piece of my heart

Mimi German

may your words be a comfort
for all who read them
for all whose lives you have touched
for all who will come to know you
even in death as i have
through your poetry

yes bird
you lead the way
your song to greet dawn

War Poem #85

i have abstained
from gods
and heathens
of war

creators
of poverty
and lovers
of sameness

i drink
from long lakes longing
and coddle down in downy wilderness
beside her shepherds
coyote
wolf
owl
and deer

i walk the wadi
dry and deep
and bathe in springs
where peace is chanted
in the chorus of stones

Mimi German

i have recognized in abstinence
that a terrorist and a government
are one and the same
and that the sun will rise
until it won't

you will keep your gods
while i'll hold my none
no kings or beasts
but vines of truth
whose berries eaten
can heal the blind

but this fog is impenetrable
there is no life after death
no raft for kindness
or ark and savior no
just peasants lost
on this earth's rock

War Poem #86

he waves his sword

at the spinning mill of terror

we will continue

    he yells

to kill

    he pounds

until we have destroyed

the messengers

of an ideology

of hatred

Mimi German

and they

      he flails his sword

will defile the women

making them too dirty to bury

then set them aflame

and call themselves

martyrs in the name

of allah

in the meantime

in the name of ideologies

        and lies

where is the forest

through all the fallen

and forgotten trees

War Poem #87

in the dream i was an israeli
a hostage to a dream

hiding beneath a house
with terrorists shooting

and like a dream
revealing itself

i realized this was uncle ike's story
pogrom stories told to us as children

about his childhood in my family's
northern village of rogachev
baranivs'kyi district
zhtomyr oblast   ukraine

uncle ike's job was to go
house to house after each attack

Mimi German

crawling fast like a little rabbit
to avoid being caught by cossacks

to see who died
and who was left
alive

he'd hover first beneath the houses
of his neighbors

scared of being seen
then shot or beheaded

and now i am uncle ike
a jew scared of what is to come

the game of revenge
ends in nightmares

War Poem #88

i do not know
which hat to wear today
or animal prints to name

so i will lick
snow from sprouting blades

of grass in fields of owls
and sorrows

Mimi German

War Poem #89

i ground myself
to the stars

the moon is tied
by gravity to earth

i am tied as a jew
to you

to your hell
in gaza

and in israel

beneath one sky
we share one earth
and the salt of seas

war leaves me nothing
but fallen

i am helpless here
in the garden of slain petals

War Poem #90

*

i have willed my self
to the mountain

our bones are none
and one

Mimi German

War Poem #91

*

laughter ceases
in the famine
of humanity

War Poem #92

humpty dumpty sat on the wall

revengefully killing

and slaughtering all

footprints eviscerate

with each bomb and blast

he thought nothing more

       than loving this war

but people then gathered

demanding humanity

they pushed humpty dumpty

down from the wall

determined to save children

and families of all

Mimi German

War Poem #93

i read the auschwitz memorials on twitter
to remember   the millions
faces   names
murdered by nazis

we don't differentiate
between which is an oak leaf and which a willow

all are dead

today's memorials read   mohammed   jawaad
mustafa   sadeel   and also   ayela   dov   dafna zohar
the list goes on and on

in israel
and in gaza

vengeance grows like moss to trees

like scorpions mating in desert heat

bullets to bodies   and bombs to buildings

war is rape   and wrath   in a future unknown

no one remembers

the history books have been burned

we have all forgotten

never to forget

Mimi German

War Poem #94

of which season do we speak

the season of spectators and ghoulish spectacles
or cold cruel seeds that float on whorish winds

the season of lapis
or of the sailor's bed of salt

the season of lonely swine
or rays rippling light on wild seas

of which season do we speak

of marauders and sewer grates
or the acceptance of grace

of monsoon madness
or the sun of frozen moons

of the clacking of heels
or the season smacking of lips

of which season do we speak

of idolatry of foraging anger
or the petals of the prairie flower

of the forlorn
or of skirts cackling in the dark

or the season of turning pages
or of the worn heart

of which season do we speak

of lovers or of gods
of life or of wars

of which season do we speak

Mimi German

War Poem #95

how delicate
the flavor
of the desert
in the negev
in sinai
in gaza

some call its fragile fruit
sabra or saber

it resists the dearth
                    of peace
and the firmament
                    of war
flowering
without politics
but feeding the thirst
of the wayfarer

i am the wayfarer
the bedouin
the wandering jew
my curling semitic tendrils
swaying in the arid search
of earth
of sea
for oneness

War Poem #96

all leaves eventually fall
from the tree

allowing light
to expose the branch

we do not fear
the tree's way

but open our hearts to it
like a lotus blossoming

in the warmth of a sun
teaching us once more

how to live like a leaf
falling from its tree

Mimi German

War Poem #97

i sit by the olive tree in my memory
toes curled to roots
reaching rivers a history's age
professing nothing
knowing only of breath
desirous of nothing
but a small bit of water

morning bathes her years
in the purple mountain sunrise
of the cold desert stunning

here I sing the stories
a bedhouin told me one night
as we smoked hash
beneath his roof of stars
at the lip of the red sea
stories of one family
with so many brothers and sisters
that they spread across this open desert
always with their tent open

for each other and each other's
others

we inhaled heaven's smoke
as he spoke

once upon a time
there were no wars here
       he said

we wove love into the sky
and that love became the river
of stars you call the milky way
the only ceiling to our home
here upon this earth and sky
indivisible and whole

once
       he went on

there was no war

Mimi German

War poem #98

'...rules are always a hindrance to free action'

-Bruno Maçães.

such a drag

these rules men create

just to ignore or break or

use as fire-blaming swords

against the wagon wheels

of one country or another

home base is secure

in its lies

and insecurities

its locks with their keys swallowed

its trillion-dollar proprieties

      for death

its airs of angelic sweetitudes

and sweeping infidelities

redemption is a lonely song

a slog on the slough golomping

along the muddy floor of history

at some point

the raft of revenge breaks

and everyone falls into the sea

Mimi German

War Poem #99

'TO BE FREE *we've got to be free of any idea of freedom'*
--Diane Di Prima

we spend so much time reaching

when we could fold

into ourselves into

each other into

the into

the soft petals of One

we could walk silently

into the sea

warmed like loaves

from the sun

bending like freedom

to taste the salt waters

of the present

our fingers wet no longer

longing

War Poem #100

i crawl
    into the universe

its pounding heart
    of lilies

its breath
    of soaring birds

waters smooth the stones
    their stories

their bitters
    flowers to heal all wounds

the talking trees
    that tell you how

flow the molten rivers
    miles deep into the pore

Mimi German

the decree of radiance

    ascends the ladder

its words

    a thousand suns

Epilogue

So what is to become of this war after the first 100 days? Nothing certain. Only a few nods to an end of the carnage. No lasting good will. No good will at all. War does not bring with it good will. Perhaps the only thing this war will bring forth is another poem or another 100 poems and if history has its way, more war.

And yet the calls for peace, the calls to cease, have accelerated. These calls are coming from the streets of Israel, from Israelis shouting down their oppressive Far-Right government, and even from the families of those who were killed or taken captive on October 7th. The plea for humanity rings the bells around the globe, from church steeples, to Gaza, to synagogues to mosques!

It is on each of us to find our voice to help end this nightmare. The compass has been broken. What have we become? All of us. What have we become?

Acknowledgements

Were it not for my teachers, I would still be hobbling through the propaganda and headlines we were handed in the 'story' telling of this war by both the Israeli government and by Hamas. My gratitude to John Bertucci for sharing his expertise on propaganda with me, for his fearless suggestions and edits in these poems, and finally, for his artwork that graces the cover of this book. To Kelly Lou O'Hanley, for her concise edits, comments. To K. Kendall, for guiding me deeper into Buddhist teachings. Blessings to Rabbi Ariel Stone for her ongoing support of my work on the streets and for leading by action, not by words alone. To my father, for teaching me how to be an honorable Jew and for providing insight into what it means to be Jewish.

To my partner, my love. Thank you for making space in our house to discuss this war on a daily basis and bearing witness with me.

About the author

Mimi German is an American poet dividing her time between living in the wilderness of Oregon's Steens Mountain and Portland, OR. She is the author of *Beneath the Gravel Weight of Stars*, *Where Grasses Bend*, and *War Poems*. German was named Oregon's Beat Poet Laureate (2023-2025) by the Beat Poetry Foundation.

Mimi left Philadelphia for NY in '82 for college. It was in NYC during the Reagan Administration that her first of a few non-violent disobedient arrests occurred. After college she joined the peace movement, Shalom Achshav (Peace Now), in Israel arriving just before the first Palestinian uprising. After returning to the US, Mimi split time between Cambridge, MA and Halifax, Nova Scotia.

In 1995, Mimi headed west to Oregon where she still resides. In 1997, Mimi was arrested again, this time on Shoshone land in Nevada with the late Chief Corbin Harney protesting against a proposed uranium dumpsite on Indian land.

In 2011 after the Fukushima nuclear disaster, Mimi started an international group called RadCast which documented citizen radiation readings post-Fukushima, from around the globe. She was often asked to speak about the reality of radioactive toxicity around the globe on national and international talk shows. She was a frequent guest on Michael J. Ruppert's show, The Lifeboat Hour and had a special weekly spot for radiation readings on Thom Hartman's show.

Mimi's poetry has been published in the New Generation Beats Anthology 2022 and in the National Beat Poetry Foundation's, Remembering Jack Kerouac On His 100th Birthday. Her work has been published in numerous publications in the US and in the UK. In 2023, Mimi was honored with the title of State of Oregon Beat Poet Laureate.

For more information **MimiGermanPoetry**.org.

About EYEPUBLISHEWE

Eye publish ewe is a brand new publishing company, founded in San Francisco. Art, music, video, poetry, and other literature will find inclusive shelter here. Quality work produced by the artists' hearts, minds, and souls rather than commercial interests will have this as a home. All are welcomed with open minds and hearts and eyes to the future. Together we will publish art for humanity's sake.

EPE titles

Where Grasses Bend: Poems from Portland to Steens Mountain in the Time of Plagues by **Mimi German** ISBN: 979-8-9870259-5-6

The Green Notebook: Poems on Family, Relationships, Spirituality, Self-Enquiry, Recovery, ACA, Disruption, Death, Walking Through the Mirror, and Cats by **John Angell Grant** ISBN: 979-8-9870259-6-3

Morning Tanka : A journal of thank you notes between lovers, California poems in the style of traditional Japanese form poetry translated by Yuri Miki by **Dane Ince** and **Mercedes Dugger** ISBN: 979-8-9898764-0-2

Crimson Stain: Poems Inspired by King's Letter from Jail, Real Life, and A Facet of Blood Diamond Culture by **Dee Allen**. ISBN: 979-8-9898764-3-3

Destiny Murder!: A Poetic Odyssey of Pulp Poems in the Beat Noir Style Concerning the Dutch Angle of Strange Dreams, Erotic, Ambivalent, Cruel and Cynical by **Dane Ince** ISBN: 979-8-9870259-8-7

EPE Titles Coming Soon

A House without Walls: Existential Journeys and Love Poems to Mexico by **Lesley Constable**

La Naturaleza del Amor: Poems in Spanish and English by **Martin Del Toro Gutierrez**